ACTUAL NORTH

LITURGICAL NORTH

2 CLOISTER The living room of the monks, the cloister comprised arcaded galleries around a garden. A small part of the arcade has been rebuilt to show its form (page 18)

1 CHURCH The nave and transepts survive from Aelred's church and originally contained the choirs of the monks and lay-brothers. The presbytery was rebuilt in the early thirteenth century, perhaps to house the abbot's shrine (pages 15–17)

8 INFIRMARY HALL AND ABBOT'S HOUSE Dating from Aelred's abbacy, the infirmary was the home of the old and sick. The abbot's house where Aelred died was attached to its west side. In the last years of the fifteenth century, Abbot John Burton rebuilt the infirmary hall as his own house (pages 28–30)

7 INFIRMARY CLOISTER A garden surrounded by arcaded galleries provided a separate cloister for the old and infirm. A section of the arcade has been rebuilt to show its form. Herbs for use in the infirmary were usually grown here (pages 28–29)

CONTENTS

INTRODUCTION

Rievaulx Abbey ranked as the most important Cistercian abbey in Britain and served as the centre for the monastic colonisation of the north of England and Scotland. Much of what is now visible of Rievaulx's buildings dates to the middle years of the twelfth century and is associated with the rule of the monastery's third abbot, Aelred.

Aelred was the most famous churchman of his day and the greatest spiritual writer that England produced in the high Middle Ages. His buildings, among the earliest and most important on any Cistercian site, provide valuable insight into Aelred's role as a patron and into the design and organisation of a great monastic institution. Later, but equally prominent, is the new monastic choir raised in the 1220s and acknowledged as one of the glories of Early English architecture. It, too, was connected with Aelred, whose gold and silver shrine was placed there.

HISTORY

The construction of Rievaulx Abbey marks the culmination of the most successful monastic reform movement in medieval Europe and the influence of Abbot Aelred. It is the expression of Aelred's own philosophy of monastic life in stone that makes the site so important.

THE CISTERCIAN ORDER

The tenth and eleventh centuries were a time of reform in the monastic world. In 1098, a group of monks left the abbey of Molesme and built a new monastery near Dijon which they called *Cistertium*. In modern French it is called Cîteaux. The new monastery's reputation for discipline and simple living attracted recruits, many of exceptional ability. Their numbers led to the establishment of sister monasteries at La Ferté in 1113, at Pontigny in 1114, and at Morimond and Clairvaux in 1115. By 1119 five more monasteries had been founded, and the time had come formally to create a new Order, to be known from *Cistertium* as the Cistercian Order.

The rapid growth of Cîteaux and its four daughter-houses required the development of a monastic philosophy. At its centre was an uncompromising insistence on poverty,

simplicity of life, and the need to separate the communities physically from the outside world. The Cistercians placed their monasteries away from other settlements, and insisted that they be self-sufficient, renouncing all cash revenues and feudal ties. Their economy was land-based. To achieve it without reliance on feudal labour, they introduced lay-brothers who could work

their estates whilst bound by monastic discipline. To the uneducated labouring and servant classes, the lay-brotherhood offered access to monastic life. The rapid growth of the order and its capacity to support itself was very much due to this economic and social concept.

To ensure the stability of these reforms, the *Charter of Love* provided the model for a central authority within the Order – a masterpiece of

St Bernard, a powerful orator, is shown preaching in the chapter house at Clairvaux

planning. Each year, every abbot was to attend a general chapter at Cîteaux to enforce collective discipline and to enact statutes by which the development and direction of the Order was to be controlled. Additionally, a cellular structure arranged abbeys in 'families' headed by Cîteaux and its four original colonies. Each new monastery was the responsibility of the house which founded it, and the abbot of that house was required to visit the colony or daughter-house annually. Papal consent was obtained to exempt Cistercian monasteries from visitation and correction by diocesan bishops, ensuring that no outside influence could distract the movement of reform.

It is difficult now to appreciate the missionary zeal of the 'new soldiers of Christ', the name they were given early in their history. Their strict discipline and asceticism appealed strongly to the aristocracy who formed the European military class. To William of Malmesbury, 'the Cistercians . . . are a model for all, a mirror for the diligent, a spur to the indolent'. Rejecting the black habits of the Benedictines and Cluniacs, the Cistercians wore undyed or white habits, and became commonly known as 'White Monks' (their lay-brothers had brown habits to distinguish them). Both were forbidden undershirts and breeches, an unheard of austerity in the colder climate of northern Europe. Their diet was sparse and unremittingly vegetarian, their life was undoubtedly harsh, and to a certain extent anti-intellectual. However it provided in the words of St Aelred of Rievaulx 'everywhere peace, everywhere serenity, and a marvellous freedom from the tumult of the world'.

The Cistercian way of life attracted men of remarkable ability to the cloister, none more so than a young Burgundian nobleman Bernard des Fontaines who entered Cîteaux with a group of his followers in 1113. Bernard progressed from novice to abbot of the daughter-house of Clairvaux in less than three years. Beginning in the 1120s, he took the Cistercian reform to a wide audience. He combined qualities of great austerity and unbounded energy with extraordinary writing and preaching gifts that made him 'the counsellor of Popes and Kings'.

FOUNDATION OF RIEVAULX

Bernard was a great organiser who saw the Cistercian reform as a missionary cause to be planned and executed with his direct interest. In 1131, he initiated plans for the foundation of Rievaulx which was to serve as the headquarters for the systematic colonisation of northern England and Scotland. Writing to Henry I of England, Bernard claimed 'In your land there is an outpost of my Lord and your Lord, an outpost he has preferred to die for than to loose. I have proposed to occupy it and I am sending men from my army who will, if it is not displeasing to you, claim it, recover it, and restore it with a strong hand.' Emissaries sent with the letter were to survey the new site and report back to Clairvaux on its suitability. Behind the letter were the actions of Walter Espec, Lord of Helmsley and a Royal Justiciar, a subject of both Henry I of England and King David of Scotland. Espec was no stranger to monastic reform. Following his King's example

St Bernard, inspired by God (the hand from the cloud), is portrayed here as teacher of young Cistercian monks

BODLEIAN LIBRARY, OXFORD

he had brought a colony of Augustinians to Kirkham in Yorkshire in 1121-22, and he was now interested in settling the militant Cistercians on his lands with the support of his two feudal lords and Thurstan, the reformist Archbishop of York. A small colony of Yorkshire monks had entered Clairvaux and perhaps we should also see their desire to return to their homeland as a further reason for the foundation of Rievaulx.

The Cistercians had already settled at Waverley in Surrey in 1128, the colony coming from l'Aumône in Normandy. Bernard grasped the chance to establish a colony in the north, almost in competition to Waverley which was to colonise southern Britain and Ireland. Both houses were to take advantage of inhospitable, sparsely populated, and uncultivated land, areas ideal for Cistercian expansion.

On 5 March 1132, twelve Clairvaux monks led by their abbot, William, who was a former master of the schools in York and had entered Clairvaux serving as Bernard's secretary, settled in the valley of the River Rye two miles from

RIGHT *An early
fourteenth-century
carving, showing one
of the post-mills that
served the abbey's
estates*

ENGLISH HERITAGE

ABOVE *Christ in Majesty, a
figure from the thirteenth-
century pulpitum or great
screen at Rievaulx*

ENGLISH HERITAGE

RIGHT *A thirteenth-century
carving from Abbey Dore in
Hereford, showing a Cistercian
monk kneeling before his abbot*

6

Espec's castle of Helmsley. The foundation of
Rievaulx Abbey as it was soon to be called
precipitated an immediate response in the
North. Particularly affected were the two great
Benedictine establishments; the cathedral priory
of Durham, and York Abbey, both rich houses
with a reputation for worldliness and thus ripe
for reform.

EARLIEST YEARS

Walter Espec provided the founding community with a small endowment, the site of the
abbey itself and the vills of Griff and Tilstone
above the valley to the north. In all, this
amounted to some 1000 acres of arable land.

In 1132 the River Rye, which ran down the
centre of the valley, formed a boundary
between the estates of Espec to the north and
Roger de Mowbray to the south. Only the area
between the river and the steeply rising valley
side was available for building, and it was here
that temporary timber buildings were raised
before the new community arrived. Building
continued well into 1132 and was overseen by
Geoffroi, a Clairvaux monk skilled in setting
out new monasteries. This was almost certainly
Geoffroi d'Ainai who also helped in the
construction of Fountains Abbey in 1133.

The new monastery at Rievaulx was
intended from the first as a mission centre, to
spread reform by the foundation of colonies or
daughter-houses. Each required an experienced
monk, normally one of the founding
community, twelve choir monks, and an
unknown number of lay-brothers. Thus the
number and frequency of their foundation gives
a clue to the expansion of the mother
community. As early as 1136 it was possible to
establish two daughter-houses; at Warden in
Bedfordshire, endowed by Espec, and at
Melrose in Scotland, endowed by Espec's friend
and lord in parts of the north, King David of
Scotland. David established a third daughter-
house at Dundrennan in 1142. From these two

houses, with the support of the Scots royal family, eight further monasteries of the Rievaulx family were established in Scotland before 1273. In 1143, a daughter-house was established at Revesby in Lincolnshire under the patronage of William de Roumare. The final daughter-house of Rufford was founded in 1146 by Roumare's son-in-law Gilbert de Gand, earl of Lincoln. Two further sites had been offered before 1138 but could not be taken up because the number of recruits was too low. The first was at Stainton in Swaledale, granted by Gilbert de Gand's father Walter;

the second was at Rushen on the Isle of Man, the gift of Olaf, King of Man. Rushen was later taken up by Furness Abbey which was more conveniently placed to oversee its settlement.

As Rievaulx expanded, Walter Espec came increasingly under the influence of the Cistercians. He had previously founded a priory of Augustine canons at Kirkham and in 1139 he tried to convert it into a daughter-house of Rievaulx. Part of the Kirkham community, led by the prior Waltheof, supported Espec, and an agreement drawn up between the two monasteries provided a new monastery and estates for those who wished to remain Augustinian. For reasons long forgotten, this agreement was not carried out and Espec was forced to climb down. As a direct result, however, he issued new foundation charters for the two monasteries that confirmed their existence and extended their land holdings. In the case of Rievaulx, this included large parts of Bilsdale and Raisdale to the west of the abbey.

This additional grant was made in 1145, and conveniently the monks had recorded all the land they had been granted before that date. In addition to Espec's original grant, they listed lands given by the King, Stephen de Mainil, Bishop William of Durham, Radulf de Novavilla, Ranulph Fitz Walter, Torphin de Alverstain, Roger de Mowbray, Bertram de Bulmer, Acaris de Tunstal, Bernard de Baliol, Robert de Lascelles, and Walter Engleram; a total of 6000 acres. While this was not an insubstantial holding, it shows that support for the founding community was slow to build up and that it came largely from the locality of the abbey.

ABOVE *A silvered-bronze scourge from Rievaulx. Self-flagellation served to mortify the flesh*

None the less the last years of William's abbacy were marked by problems with neighbours. One such occurred in 1143 with Roger de Mowbray who had settled a group of Savigniac monks at Old Byland on the opposite side of the Rye. Since the two monasteries followed slightly different time-tables, their bells disturbed each other, creating a situation 'which was not fitting and could not be endured'. After discussions the Byland monks agreed to move to a new site in 1147 at about the time the Savigniacs were absorbed by the Cistercian order. Subsequent good relations between the two houses, especially during the rules of Abbots Roger of Byland (1142-96) and Aelred of Rievaulx (1147-67), led to agreement about the course of the Rye which was the boundary between the two houses. The outcome was that Rievaulx was able to change the course of the river to the south side of the valley, thereby greatly enlarging the area

ABOVE *Corbel bracket from Rievaulx, carved with a triple face*

7

The early thirteenth-century presbytery was light and colourful, a fit setting for the high altar and St Aelred's Shrine. A reconstruction by Peter Dunn

available for the precinct and allowing Rievaulx to control the river, essential for the development of the abbey's economy.

Abbot William's died in 1145 and his place as abbot was taken by Maurice, a scholar of distinction trained at Durham where he had been sub-prior and who contemporaries compared to Bede. After 18 months in office he resigned to become abbot of Fountains. In his place, the community had elected Aelred, then abbot of the daughter-house of Revesby.

AELRED

For the 400 hundred years of its existence, Rievaulx was dominated by the life and reputation of Aelred. Drawn to the abbey two years after its foundation, he rose rapidly from monk to novice master and from novice master to the founding abbot of Rievaulx's daughter-house at Revesby. Four years later in 1147, at the age of 37, Aelred became abbot of

Rievaulx. By that time, Aelred was the most prominent religious figure in England. Besides being acquainted with the most powerful men in the land, he was a leader of great shrewdness and skill who made Rievaulx the largest monastic establishment in the country. Aelred was also a master stylist of written Latin and the pre-eminent theological author of his age in England.

Aelred was born in 1110 at Hexham into an old, well-connected English family with ties going back to the golden age of Northumbria. Many of his immediate ancestors were associated with the church of Durham and the cult of its saint, Cuthbert. Educated in the Latin classics and the early church fathers, he won a place at the age of 15 in the household of the Scottish king, David. He rose quickly within the King's court and was early marked out for high ecclesiastical office.

At 24 Aelred was sent by King David on an official visit to negotiate with Archbishop Thurstan of York. On his return to Scotland, the road north took him along the ridge overlooking the valley of the Rye. Aelred paused to look down on the new monastery's temporary wooden buildings and there experienced the call to join Rievaulx. It was a triumphant moment for the community. Aelred was no ordinary postulant; his high social standing and prestige made him by far the most prominent figure to throw in his lot with the new reform movement and his connections to the Scottish court promised future patronage for Rievaulx.

Only a little is known of Aelred's early years at Rievaulx. He shared fully in the life of the community including the required manual work. In Aelred's case this involved the breaking and gathering of stone for the permanent buildings then being raised to replace the original timber ones. In 1142, Aelred was sent to Rome as Rievaulx's delegate to persuade the reform-minded Pope Innocent II to oppose the election of a new Archbishop of York. His journey through France took him to Clairvaux, the mother-house of Rievaulx, where he met Bernard who insisted, among other things, that Aelred undertake a book on charity.

On Aelred's return to Yorkshire the community appointed him novice master, a position of particular importance during a time of prodigious growth. For the novices Aelred completed the work urged on him by Bernard, the *Mirror of Charity*, which remains the best known and admired of his more than 20 books. It was written to help the novices understand the qualities and conditions of their new life and centred on the relationship of the individual to the community. The book argues calmly for the Cistercians' early views on a large range of matters including poverty in architecture and furnishings.

A fuller picture of Aelred as leader emerges from the four years that followed which were spent establishing the colony of Revesby in Lincolnshire. The task called on all of Aelred's diplomatic and fund-raising skills. It included the forced resettlement of villagers dispossessed by the monks in establishing the new abbey's estates (a practice for which the Cistercians were more than once responsible), and the ceaseless efforts to recruit men and to enlist the help of patrons.

Aelred's election as abbot of Rievaulx in 1147 launched the most brilliant period of his career. Much of the information on these years comes from the *Life of Aelred* written by the infirmarer at Rievaulx, Walter Daniel. Although the *Life* was not so much biography as hagiography, and as such designed to serve as the first step in the process of canonisation, it none the less informs us about his personality and permits a glimpse into the life of a major religious figure in the medieval church. The latter included incessant travels, demands as writer and correspondent, and unremitting calls as preacher, conciliator, and counsellor.

As abbot of a house with five daughter-houses Aelred made yearly official visitations that took him as far north as Dundrennan in south-west Scotland and as far south as Warden in Bedfordshire. He was also required to attend the annual General Chapter of the Order at Cîteaux in southern Burgundy. Outside the abbey, Aelred was on constant call: in 1147 he arbitrated a dispute involving Durham, in 1151 another between the Norman reform movement of Savigny and Furness, and in 1152 a third within the Gilbertine Order. In 1155 he preached at Hexham on the occasion of the translation of relics, in 1163 he participated in the council at Westminster that settled the controversy between St Albans and Lincoln and later in the same year preached at the translation of the canonised remains of Edward the Confessor at Westminster Abbey. In 1164 he attested an agreement between the reform movements of Cîteaux and Sempringham. At the same time Aelred included within his correspondence (involving over 300 letters) King Henry II, Louis VI of France, and Pope Alexander III. This wide, cosmopolitan circle centred on Aelred was reflected within his community; a contemporary wrote that '. . . to Rievaulx (came) from foreign nations and distant lands a stream of monks who

needed brotherly mercy and true compassion, and there they found peace and sanctity without which no man can see God'.

The *Life* also contains much about the last 10 years of Aelred's life and the illness that frequently plagued him. This caused the order's General Chapter to grant permission for him to live outside the dormitory, an exception which led to the construction of the attached but separate quarters linked to the infirmary, the 'long house'. So severe was Aelred's illness that some days he was reduced to lying on the ground in front of a fire 'twisted in pain like a sheet of parchment' while on others his skin became so sensitive to touch that it required a man at each corner of a sheet to carry him to relieve himself or to the baths to reduce his pain.

Death came on 12 January 1167 and according to custom Aelred was buried in the chapter house next to abbot William, the abbey's founder. Within a few years procedures were instituted to secure his canonisation. At some time in the second quarter of the thirteenth century his body was removed from the chapter house and placed in a gold and silver shrine behind the high altar in the new presbytery which was almost certainly built to receive it. There it remained as the focus of the church and community until it was destroyed in 1536.

LATER HISTORY OF RIEVAULX

Because no chronicle survives, and because Cistercian abbeys were exempt from visitation by diocesan bishops, very little is known of the history of Rievaulx after the death of Aelred.

By the end of the thirteenth century, the abbey was deeply in debt. Rievaulx was not unique in this, for many of the northern monasteries had been building substantially and buying lands in the first half of the century with money often borrowed against future income. Speculation in wool, one of the staples of the Cistercian economy, was widespread. Although the wool yield was by no means certain, it was tempting to anticipate income several years in advance, a practice encouraged by the great continental wool-merchants. However, an epidemic of sheep-scab in 1280 caused a serious drop in production.

In 1279, Rievaulx was already in debt to Florentine merchants and others, and the king appointed Alexander de Kirketon to sort out its debts. In 1288, the abbey was again taken into royal protection, with the Bishop of Durham appointed as keeper. The extent of the debt, blamed on the sheep murrain, is unknown, but

Aelred, Abbot of Rievaulx 1147-67, from an illuminated initial in a Cistercian manuscript

BIBLIOTHEQUE MUNICIPALE, DONAI

9

Fountains Abbey, trading on a greater scale, saw its debts rise from £900 in 1274 to the catastrophic figure of £6373 in 1291.

The early fourteenth century saw local troubles overshadowed by national disaster. The English defeat at the Battle of Bannockburn in 1314 and the over-running of the north by the Scots army was disastrous for many monasteries whose estates were looted and granges burned. Rievaulx featured briefly in the aftermath of this disaster. King Edward II was staying at Rievaulx in 1322 when he was surprised by the Scots army at Shaws Moor where the Battle of Byland was fought. Defeated, the English retreated to York, and the Scots plundered Rievaulx before they withdrew. The extent of the damage is unknown. The disruption of the abbey's estates resulted in the demise of the lay-brothers who were traditionally drawn from them. This necessitated a change in the economy which shifted from grange farming to manorial farming and tenancies. Income would never be so great as it had been in the mid-thirteenth century, with the result that the number of choir-monks was substantially reduced. Compounding these problems in the mid-century was the devastation of the Black Death in 1348-49. By 1381-82 the community comprised the abbot, fourteen monks, and three lay-brothers.

Monastic life at Rievaulx in the fourteenth and fifteenth centuries appears to have been unexceptional, though the buildings suggest that it was becoming more comfortable. The Cistercians began to adopt a meat diet from the fourteenth century and small apartments for individual monks became commonplace. Yet towards the end of the fifteenth century, the steady decline in the number of monks slowed, and this small renaissance is marked by the building of a substantial abbot's house by Abbot John Burton in the last decade of the century. The house marks the abbot's status but it also indicates the aspirations of the community. Although there is no record of the abbot of Rievaulx being granted the honour of wearing a mitre, the later abbots almost certainly enjoyed the privileges of quasi-episcopal status, for among the abbey's possessions in 1538 was a mitre of paste (i.e. base metal) set with pearls.

BEGINNING OF THE END

In 1530, Edward Kirby was elected abbot. A conservative churchman, he is unlikely to have supported the changes that were about to sweep the church. In 1532, Henry VIII declared himself supreme head, below God, of the church in England and the following years saw great pressure for the reform and ultimate destruction of monastic institutions. Kirby soon provoked the king's displeasure when it was discovered in 1533 that he had written a letter that questioned Henry VIII's authority to interfere in church matters.

The king required William Thirsk, abbot of Fountains and commissary of the abbot of Cîteaux to enquire into the matter along with royal commissioners. Thirsk would have nothing to do with the allegations, finding no fault, an action that was to lead to his own downfall three years later. The commissioners, however, deprived Kirby of his abbacy. Thomas Manners, later to become Earl of Rutland, was both patron of the abbey as the lineal successor of Walter Espec, and an active supporter of the king. He was granted royal licence to require the election of a new abbot, and Abbot Thirsk and Abbot John of Byland were commanded to arrange this in September 1533. Abbot Thirsk wisely pleaded more important royal business elsewhere, and Abbot John alone had the responsibility of securing the election of a new abbot of Rievaulx. Out of the community of 23, only seven were prepared to proceed to a new election, and none of the monks, including the prior, believed that Kirby had been deposed lawfully as required by the statutes of the order. In November, however, the king issued a further instruction to proceed with the election, and Rowland Blyton, abbot of Rufford, was finally installed on 8 December, Edward Kirby officiating. Part of the deal whereby Kirby acquiesced to Blyton's succession was the granting of a pension of £44 a year for life, an agreement which Blyton strenuously refused to honour.

The end of the abbey was rapidly approaching. In 1536, the majority of monasteries with an annual income of less than £200 had been suppressed, resulting in the north in the outbreak of a rebellion, the Pilgrimage of Grace. Blyton kept his community out of this, ensuring its survival for a short while. However, a visitation of the greater monasteries began in January 1538 with the express purpose of securing their surrender to the crown. It was a lengthy process, and on 3 December 1538 Abbot Blyton and 21 monks surrendered their monastery.

The site of the abbey and its home estates in Ryedale and Bilsdale were granted to Thomas Manners, Earl of Rutland. The current owner is Lord Feversham of Duncombe Park, although the site is maintained and managed by English Heritage.

Stamp used to identify the king's lead from the demolition of Rievaulx in 1538-39

LAY-BROTHERS' RANGE

CLOISTER

REFECTORY

TANNERY

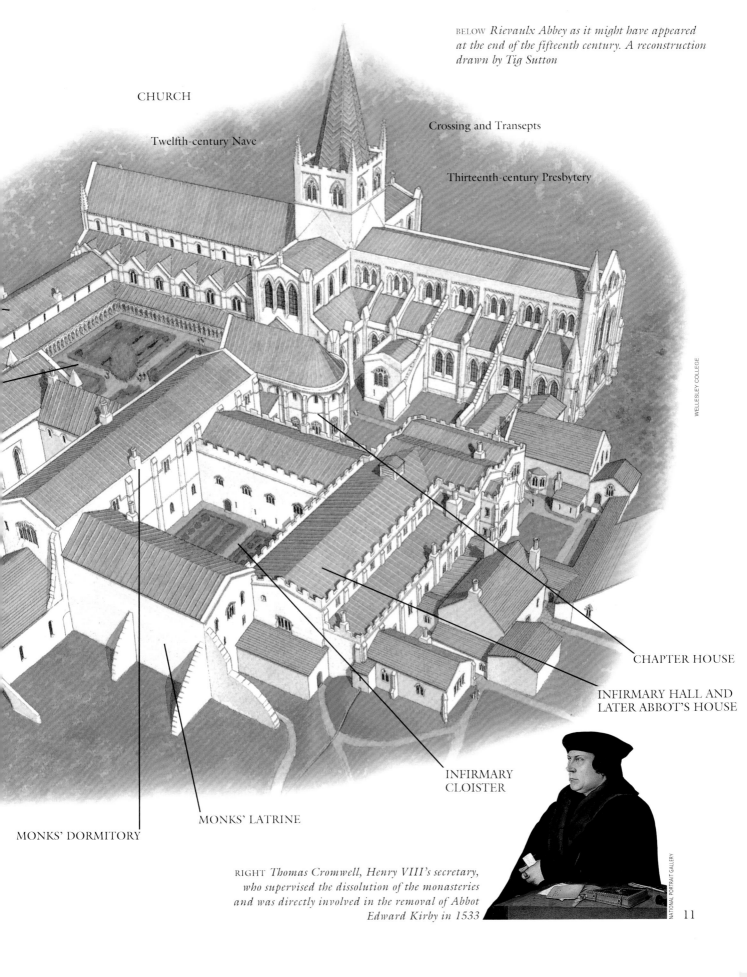

BELOW *Rievaulx Abbey as it might have appeared at the end of the fifteenth century. A reconstruction drawn by Tig Sutton*

CHURCH

Twelfth-century Nave

Crossing and Transepts

Thirteenth-century Presbytery

CHAPTER HOUSE

INFIRMARY HALL AND LATER ABBOT'S HOUSE

INFIRMARY CLOISTER

MONKS' LATRINE

MONKS' DORMITORY

RIGHT *Thomas Cromwell, Henry VIII's secretary, who supervised the dissolution of the monasteries and was directly involved in the removal of Abbot Edward Kirby in 1533*

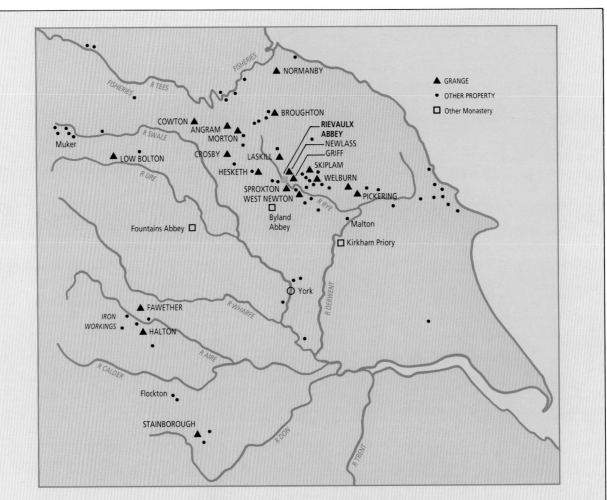

THE ABBEY'S ESTATES

FOLLOWING WALTER ESPEC'S second foundation charter of 1145, many estates were granted to the abbey, often in fairly small blocks. It was the astute acquisition and consolidation of these holdings, particularly from 1147 to 1188, that produced a coherent estate capable of sustaining a large community. There were only minor additions to the estate after the early thirteenth century. The general form of the estates can be reconstructed from the abbey's cartulary, a collection of charters made in the late twelfth century, though it is clear from other sources that this is incomplete.

The principal estates lay to the north and east of the abbey, centred on the home granges of Griff, Newlass, Bilsdale, Laskill and Sproxton, with further granges at Hesketh, Skiplam, and Pickering; to the north-west across the Hambleton Hills the granges of Angram, Crosby, Morton, and Broughton exploited holdings in the Vale of Mowbray, and

lands in the the lower Tees valley was controlled from Normanby. In west Yorkshire, industrial granges were established at Faweather and Halton near Bingley, and in south Yorkshire at Stainborough. Some estate centres consisted of manors, though they were run in the same way as granges. Substantial holdings on the Tees, which ran in parallel with the estates of Fountains and Byland provided fisheries and horse-breeding. Wool was exploited in the Vale of Pickering and the northern flank of the Yorkshire Wolds, in the upper reaches of Swaledale centred on Muker, and in the Aire valley in the vicinity of Heaton. Major ironworks were acquired in the later twelfth century in Calderdale at Flockton and to the south of Barnsley. In all, the abbey was provided with a mixed economy that compared well with any other great monastery in the North. The greater part of the land held in 1250 was still held in 1538 when the house was suppressed.

DESCRIPTION OF THE ABBEY

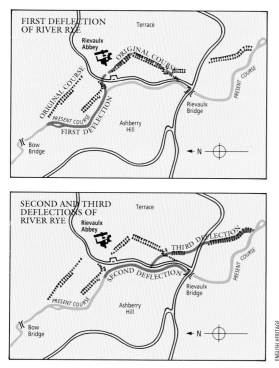

FIRST DEFLECTION OF RIVER RYE

Terrace
Rievaulx Abbey
ORIGINAL COURSE
ORIGINAL COURSE
PRESENT COURSE
PRESENT COURSE
FIRST DEFLECTION
Ashberry Hill
Rievaulx Bridge
Bow Bridge
← N

SECOND AND THIRD DEFLECTIONS OF RIVER RYE

Terrace
Rievaulx Abbey
THIRD DEFLECTION
SECOND DEFLECTION
PRESENT COURSE
PRESENT COURSE
Ashberry Hill
Rievaulx Bridge
Bow Bridge
← N

ENGLISH HERITAGE

THE SITE

Long hailed for the beauty of its setting, the abbey sits in a turn of the narrow valley of the Rye. Ledged one third up the valley floor on a series of man-made terraces, Rievaulx commands broad views to the east and west over lush green meadows which in turn are framed by the tree-clad walls of the valley. The picture of well-ordered, verdant plenty is the result of two fundamental changes to the landscape. The first was undertaken by the monks in the early years of Rievaulx's settlement. Formerly, the river ran through the centre of the valley and the original course may be traced in earthworks by the visitor prepared to walk the former outer areas of the precinct. Between 1145 and 1185 the monks engineered three deflections of the river so that now its course skirts the valley's southern rim. It was moved to create space for the abbey. The second change is much more recent. In the course of clearing the site of fallen debris,

particularly between 1920 and 1950, more than 50,000 tonnes of debris from the site were spread over adjacent fields to level up meadows and produce a clean-lined, regular, park-like appearance which makes it harder to visualise the original layout of the monastery.

The buildings now in the care of English Heritage represent only the nucleus of the abbey. Fewer than half the 72 buildings listed at the suppression in 1538 can be traced and the 15 acres (6ha) of the present site are all that remain of the 92 acres (37ha) which were originally enclosed within the precinct wall. To the east and west of the monument as we now see it lay about 35 acres (14ha) respectively; these contained the abbey's courts, meadows, orchards, gardens, fishponds, mills, service and industrial buildings. None of these survives above ground. Yet they need to be added in the imagination in order to grasp the original extent of the abbey which at the height of its history formed the living quarters for about 400 men.

ABOVE LEFT *Deflections of the River Rye in the twelfth century*

ABOVE *The abbey church before conservation work began in 1919. The foreground comprises mounds of fallen debris from the nave*

13

TOUR OF THE ABBEY

The present day entrance bears no relationship to the original access to the abbey which was entered to the north-west of the abbey by a great gatehouse close to the parish church, once the abbey's gate chapel. From the admission point and shop, follow the path towards the museum. From the museum, walk along the north side of the church until you come to the porch at the west end of the nave. You are now close to the original access.

Normally, monastic churches have an east to west alignment. At Rievaulx this is not the case and the church is aligned from south-east to north-west. Since at least the early sixteenth century, Rievaulx's buildings have been described as having a traditional east–west axis, and this guide does likewise.

CHURCH

The church was the most important building of the monastery, where the monks were required to maintain a daily round of seven services and to hear Mass. In plan it was cruciform, with nave, transepts, and presbytery. The surviving ruins date from two periods; one in the 1150s, the second in the 1220s.

The church is entered through the remains of a porch or **Galilee**, a characteristic feature of Cistercian churches. Built originally in the 1150s, it was remodelled on at least two occasions with solid walls which replaced the open arcade that would originally have fronted it. The Galilee was a popular burial place for lay patrons until the later thirteenth century and traces remain of eight graves. A tomb on the north side of the door into the nave carries the name of Isabel de Roos who died in 1264. To the south of the church door is the coped grave-cover of one Jordan.

The **nave** and **transepts** represent one of the oldest extant Cistercian churches in Europe. Begun during Aelred's abbacy, it was probably completed within five years. Unfortunately the nave is heavily ruined, though the transepts survive on their north, west, and south faces to almost full height and provide a good impression of the remainder of the building. The nave was divided from its aisles by an arcade of slightly pointed arches which sprang from boldly splayed piers with tall square bases and shallow capitals. The aisles were vaulted in the manner of the Cistercian abbey churches in Burgundy, with barrel vaults which carried the profile of the arches back to the aisle walls. The twelfth-century nave, unlike the later presbytery, was of simple two-storey construction, without a triforium. The nave roof survived until 1538,

when it was described as a painted ceiling. From the start, almost certainly, the underside of the timber roof structure was boarded to give the impression of a vault. There was clearly an intention to reduce the architecture of the Rievaulx church to the simplest form possible. Building materials were also simple, with rubble used for the greater part and dressed stone restricted to doors, piers, arches, angles, and string courses. The whole of the structure was plastered inside and out, white-limed, and painted with false joints to represent fine quality masonry.

The model for this church was probably Clairvaulx (the monastery from which Rievaulx was founded) built between 1135 and 1145 during the abbacy of Bernard and known to Aelred. It certainly reflects the plan and functional austerity typical of the family of Clairvaulx during Bernard's lifetime.

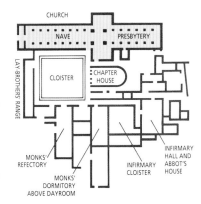

The nave of nine bays and the crossing in fact housed two separate churches. In the nave was the lay-brothers' choir that occupied the second to seventh bays and was closed to the east by a rood screen. The monks' choir occupied the last bay of the nave and all of the crossing and was closed to the west by the pulpitum screen. These two areas were divided from each other by the retrochoir where the old and infirm could sit during services. The only communication between the two churches was in the aisles which served as corridors divided from the central area by low walls against which were set the lay-brothers' and monks' stalls. Each of the transepts had three square-ended chapels, demolished in the thirteenth century,

ABOVE *Seen from the crossing, the monks' new church was one of the most elaborate to be built in England by the Cistercians*

FACING PAGE *The building of the new presbytery marked a softening in the Cistercians' attitude to architecture, in contrast to the austerity of the earlier church* 15

and to the east of the crossing an unaisled presbytery of two bays housed the main altar.

The nave remained the province of the lay-brothers until the fourteenth century, though the monks began to encroach on their space. From the middle years of the fourteenth century, chapels were inserted into the four eastern bays of the aisles, four on the north side and three on the south. Their altars and fittings survive for the most part, and the sockets for their screens can be seen on the nave piers and side walls. In their present form they date to about 1400. Abbot Henry Burton was buried in the eastern chapel on the south side after 1429. With the disappearence of the lay-brothers in the second half of the fourteenth century, their choir was cleared away, leaving the nave free for processional use. It was brought up to date at the end of the fourteenth century when its windows were replaced with fashionable traceried lights filled with pictorial glass of good quality. As part of the same restoration a door was inserted from the south aisle into the west alley of the cloister and an exquisite Holy Water stoup was provided next to the eastern cloister door.

In the early thirteenth century, the community rebuilt the eastern parts of the church in a very different style. Beginning at the east end, a new **presbytery** of seven bays and of three storeys was constructed, covered by masonry vaults. Since the old presbytery was not dismantled until the new one was well advanced, accurate measurement from the east side of the crossing to the line of the new east wall was not possible and the new east wall was built too far to the west. As a result the westernmost bay of the new presbytery was narrower than the other six bays and the design of the triforium or middle stage had to be altered to make it fit. The use of heavily detailed architectural decoration was very un-Cistercian in character: the arcade piers were clustered; the arches heavily moulded; and the bays divided by shafts which rose through the triforium storey to carry the high vault. At clerestory level a wall passage, fronted by tall arches and flanked by lower blind arches, framed twin lancet windows. The buttresses of both aisle walls were carried up as flying buttresses to support the high vault.

The eastern bay of the new presbytery was

Flying buttressess supported the high vault of the presbytery

ENGLISH HERITAGE

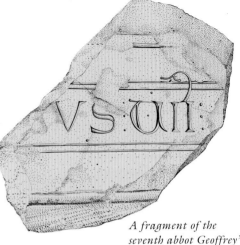

A fragment of the seventh abbot Geoffrey's tomb

fitted out with five chapels ranged along the east wall with one in each aisle and three in the central vessel. The three central ones contained images of St John the Baptist, St John the Evangelist, and Our Lady in 1538. The second bay from the east was an ambulatory serving these chapels and it is here that a shrine was raised to St Aelred, perhaps the reason for building the new presbytery. Between the second piers of the arcade was a screen with a loft above from which the shrine could be better observed. Against the west side of this screen the high altar was placed. Its stone top still lies on the presbytery floor. The space around the altar was enclosed by a stone arcade of which only the foundations now remain.

From the last years of the thirteenth century, patrons were buried outside this screen between the piers, and the substructure of a double grave, that of John de Ros who died in 1393 and his wife Maria who died in the following year can be seen to the south of the high altar. Many fragmentary tomb effigies were found when the eastern arm of the church was excavated in 1919 and there must have been tombs between each of the piers and perhaps more in the open area in front of the high altar, including Thomas de Ros, lord of Helmsley and patron of the house, who was buried at the centre of the choir in 1384. In the fifth bay from the east were two steps down to the level of the monks' choir which was moved into the new presbytery on its completion. The

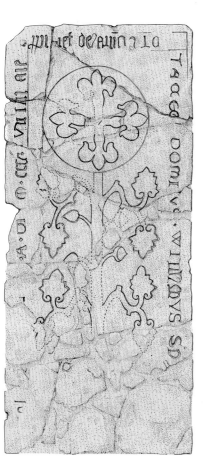

foundations of the choir stalls can still be seen in the floor, and sockets in the eastern crossing piers show the location of the new pulpitum and its loft. In the south aisle was a great timber press for vestments and a cupboard for service books, close to a sacristy added in the fourteenth century. In the second bay from the east, a door was provided to give access to the new presbytery from the infirmary to the south.

A new tower was built at the **crossing**. Its eastern piers were of new construction but the western piers simply clad the mid-twelfth-century crossing piers which can still be seen. The tower was not designed as a lantern to throw light into the central part of the church, for it had a vault immediately above its arches. Above the vault was a bell-chamber and above that a timber steeple which fell before 1538 into the south transept where its timbers, lead covering and bells remained after the suppression.

The **transepts** were rebuilt on their eastern sides to match the elevations of the new presbytery, with two chapels in each, new windows were provided in the heightened gable walls, and a clerestory added to the western side. The work is of poorer quality than in the presbytery and gives every impression of being hurried. Although the new transept chapels were vaulted to match the aisles of the presbytery, the transepts themselves had a timber roof. The junction of the old and new work is marked by a dramatic change in the colour and texture of the stone used. A new door was inserted into the gable wall of the north transept to provide access to the convent cemetery that lay to the north and east of the new presbytery.

The south transept retains a fragment of the tile mosaic floor that the transepts and eastern arm was fitted with in the 1230s. In its south-west corner is the night door from the monks' dormitory, close to which was placed a clock in an elaborate wooden case that remained until 1538. A slot in the northern pier of the transept arcade held a bracket that carried a statue of St Christopher, so placed that it could be seen by the monks as they came into church for the night services from the adjoining dormitory.

Leave the church by the eastern processional door where ten steps take you down to the lower level of the cloister.

TOP LEFT *Gravestone of Abbot William Spenser* LOWER LEFT *Grave-marker of Abbot Henry Burton*

ENGLISH HERITAGE (DRAWINGS BY JUDITH DOBIE)

ABOVE *Gravestone of the twentieth abbot Peter, buried in the chapter house*

BELOW *A fragment of a tomb from the church. The partial inscription reads '…M ORAT(E)' – pray (for the soul of)*

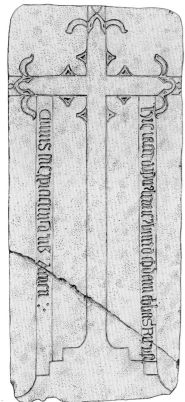

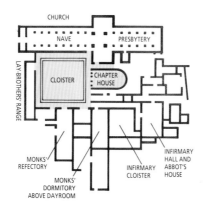

A corner of the cloister arcade has been rebuilt from fallen masonry to show its form

CLOISTER

The **cloister**, which was laid out before Aelred became abbot, is 140ft (42.5m) square and lies on the south side of the church. It comprised a square garth or garden surrounded by broad alleys enclosed by an open arcade. A section of the arcade which dates from the 1150s has been re-erected from fallen fragments in the north-west corner. Evidence for the timber roof can be seen in the walls of the church and on the south side of the cloister. The central space enclosed by the cloister alleys was not originally grassed. Aelred mentions flowers and fruit trees there in the 1160s in his treatise on friendship.

The cloister alleys formed the monks' living space and provided access to the monastery's principal rooms for work and business. In the north alley desks served for the reading of books and the copying of manuscripts; in the west alley the novices studied; in the south alley piped water provided for the monks' laundry and for washing prior to meals.

LIBRARY AND VESTRY

A large round-headed recess against the south transept contained the **cupboard** in which were stored books for reading in the cloister, and to its south, a square recess in the cloister wall once held a wax-coated tablet on which were listed the names of monks with special duties for the week, a very rare survival.

Next to the south transept lay a narrow room, its floor 4ft (1.3m) below the level of the cloister alley. It was covered with a vault and divided into two rooms. Contemporary with the construction of the church, the room served in its west part as the **library**, entered from the cloister by a wide doorway, later narrowed, and in the east part as a **vestry** reached down steps from a blocked original door in the transept gable. Above this room a second vestry was reached by a door in the transept chapel. To the west lay the passage to the dormitory from the church.

CHAPTER HOUSE

Next to the library and vestries was the **chapter house**, so called because a chapter of the rule of St Benedict was read here daily before the convent turned to discuss its spiritual and social business. Here, too, the early abbots were buried, and on high feasts the convent assembled for a sermon. Constructed at the same time as Aelred's church and second only in importance to it, the chapter house displays an architectural sophistication in strong contrast to the church.

In plan the chapter house is a rectangular room with an apse at its east end, enclosed on all sides by an arcade that supported a clerestory. It is unique in a Cistercian context. It was entered from the cloister by a centrally placed door flanked by round-headed windows of two lights, and there were two further plain, round-headed doors leading into the north and south aisles. Both of these doors have a porter's seat cut into their southern side. The western bay formed a vestibule which was vaulted at a lower level than the others to allow the passage from the monks' dormitory to pass over the chapter house. All the aisles were covered with rib vaults. The western piers of the arcade were made up of drums, but all the others have

monolithic shafts, and all carried elaborate scalloped capitals, one of which remains in place. The design of the building was changed during construction. On the south side, scars show the earlier positioning of the wall shafts of the aisle vault, and there are changes elsewhere. The alterations were originally hidden by white-limed plaster, which was painted with simple masonry patterns.

Within the arcade, three tiers of stone benching were provided for the monks to sit on. In the three western bays the seating appears to be of twelfth-century date, but in the apse it was rebuilt in the late fourteenth century. At this time the aisle was removed from the apse and the arcade blocked up and buttressed. The aisles with their separate doors serve no purpose in the normal use of a Cistercian chapter house, and it has been suggested that this space was provided to enable the lay-brothers to hear sermons, an innovation that would have been typical of Aelred. With the demise of the lay-brothers in the fourteenth century, the aisle became redundant and was partially removed.

Inset in the floor are seven grave slabs and three coffins which have lost their covers. All of these are the graves of abbots, but only three can be identified: William Punchard, the sixth abbot who died in 1203; Peter, the twenty-second abbot who died about 1307; and John, the twenty-seventh abbot who died about 1327. The cover stones of six further graves can be seen in the cloister alley outside the chapter house, the usual location of important lay burials from the twelfth century.

An early wall with a door in it running below the west wall of the chapter house can still be seen below a grill in the cloister alley. A second wall is known to run parallel to this one, 25ft (7.67m) to the east. These are part of the first monastery built by Abbot William. They demonstrate that Aelred's chapter house and the buildings to its south represent a rebuilding and are not the first stone buildings to be erected in the east range.

Aelred's chapter house (right foreground) was perhaps the most remarkable of his buildings

19

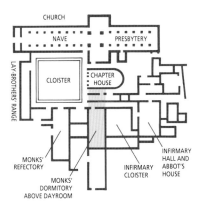

SHRINE OF ST WILLIAM

 IN THE MID-THIRTEENTH CENTURY an elaborate shrine of Rievaulx's founding abbot, William (1132-45) was inserted into the window on the north side of the chapter house door. It could be approached from inside the building and from the cloister alley. In form, the shrine had two stages, on the upper of which and below an elaborately vaulted canopy was placed the saint's coffin or reliquary. A detached fragment of the slab on which the reliquary stood was inscribed 'SCS WILLMUS Abbas' (St William the abbot), and a second stone had been inscribed in a fifteenth century hand 'Willmus primus Abbas Rievall' (William, first abbot of Rievaulx). Originally he had been buried in the chapter house floor, with Aelred buried next to him. An inscription on the inner sill of the window to the south of the chapter house door may provide the date of his translation: 'A° MCCL V KAL M' (In the year 1250 on the fifth day of March), the 118th anniversary of the abbey's foundation.

Abbot William's shrine (below) stands between the chapter house and the cloister. A reconstruction (above) has been drawn from excavated evidence by Peter Dunn

PARLOUR, DAY-STAIR, AND TREASURY

On the south side of the chapter house, a long narrow room forms a passage through the range. Along its side walls are stone benches, and its ceiling was vaulted. This room was the **parlour**, where monks might talk to each other for a short period in the day without breaking the rule of silence required in the cloister. Later than the chapter house because its construction required the removal of three buttresses on the south side of that building, the two buildings are not very far apart in date. A door at the east end of the south wall (now blocked) led into the treasury which lay below the twelfth-century day-stairs to the dormitory above. The present access is modern, through the breach in the back of a cupboard.

South of the parlour and extending out into the east alley of the cloister was the **monks' day-stair** to their dormitory, of which the lowest steps remain. Below it was a narrow room with a barrel vaulted ceiling and a tall round-headed window in its east wall that retains evidence for both bars and shutters. This room could only be entered originally from the parlour, though a door was inserted in its east wall at the end of the fifteenth century to provide access from the abbot's apartments and the door to the parlour walled up. Small cupboards were provided in the walls. This secure and fireproof room was the **treasury** where valuables belonging to the convent and local landowners could be safely stored.

PASSAGE AND DAYROOM

To the south of the day-stair, a **passage** through the range led to the infirmary buildings. A door in the south wall leads to the **dayroom** where some of the monks practised manual labour within the confines of the

20

cloister. Because of the site terracing, its floor is 5ft (1.52m) below the cloister.

The dayroom was covered with groined vaults in four and a half double bays carried on piers down the centre of the room and on plain corbels set in the side walls. A substantial amount of fallen vault was recovered when this room was excavated, including stones set at the vault apex which were fitted with an iron ring for the suspension of lamps. The piers down the centre of the room alternate between cylindrical piers of coursed stone and monolithic piers with detached angle shafts. A round-headed window lit each bay of the side walls, those on the west being set high up under the vault because of a covered passage on the outside face of the wall. Today, the room has two fireplaces but neither was an original feature of the room. The

earliest, in the second bay of the west wall, dates perhaps to the 1170s when the room was temporarily used as the warming house. Opposite, the projecting fireplace in the third bay with square lamp brackets on each side is fourteenth century. Two doors lead from this room, one on the west side to a yard, and a second in the south-east corner to the novices' room. Two further doors are provided in the south wall where a narrow chamber with a half barrel vault contains a large latrine set over the abbey's main sewer. This latrine served the dayroom and cloister.

Originally, the east range continued for another 100ft beyond the south wall of the latrine, where because of the terracing of the site it was three storeys high. The southern part of the range is described on page 27.

Seen from the east, the scale of the abbey's buildings built on three terraces can be appreciated in this aerial photograph

21

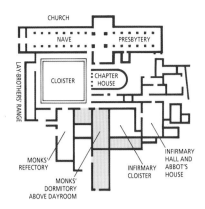

CHURCH
NAVE · PRESBYTERY
CLOISTER · CHAPTER HOUSE
LAY-BROTHERS' RANGE
MONKS' REFECTORY
MONKS' DORMITORY ABOVE DAYROOM
INFIRMARY CLOISTER
INFIRMARY HALL AND ABBOT'S HOUSE

DORMITORY

Decorative floor tiles were used in most of the abbey's buildings from the thirteenth to fifteenth centuries

The **monks' dormitory** occupied the upper floor of the east range from the south wall of the chapter house to the south end of the range, a vast room originally 245ft (75m) long and 34ft (10.3m) wide, large enough to have housed the 140 monks recorded here in the 1160s. Its floor level is marked by an ashlar levelling course in the inner face of the side walls. If the same arrangements existed at Rievaulx as are recorded at Clairvaulx, the monks' beds were arranged along the walls and the centre of the room was filled with clothes presses.

A tall round-headed window occupied each bay of the side walls, best seen now on the west side. In the late fourteenth century the dormitory was shortened by 99ft (30m) and a cross wall built on the line of the south wall of the dayroom latrine below. This new wall can be recognised by the quality of its masonry which contrasts strongly with the rubble work of the twelfth-century range. The shortening of the dormitory indicates that the number of choir monks had fallen substantially but there are also indications of a rising standard of comfort. Almost certainly the room was partitioned into individual cells, and in the east wall, at least one of the dormitory windows was replaced by a larger opening. At the south end of the east wall (and at the centre of the twelfth-century range) are two doors that led to the monks' latrine block which projects to the east of the range, one to enter and one to leave.

LATRINE BLOCK AND NOVICES' ROOM

Best seen from the south end of the dayroom is the three-storey block that contained the novices' room above a cellar at ground floor, and the monks' latrine at first floor level. The southern side of the building contains the main sewer which is divided from the basement and ground floor by a wall.

The **cellarage** in the basement, unusually provided here because of the way the site was terraced, was covered with a vault, the springings of which remain. A long and dark room, it was lit by three tiny windows high up in its north wall with light-shafts constructed in the vault itself. An original cross-wall divided the main area of cellarage to the west from a smaller room to the east and contained a round-headed door. A door in the north-west corner of the main cellar led by way of a timber stair into the infirmary cloister.

ENGLISH HERITAGE (TILE DRAWINGS BY KAREN GUFFOGG)

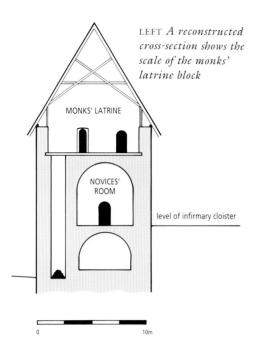

LEFT *A reconstructed cross-section shows the scale of the monks' latrine block*

MONKS' LATRINE

NOVICES' ROOM

level of infirmary cloister

0   10m

The **novices' room** on the ground floor, at the same level as the monks' dayroom and entered from it, was a very fine apartment, with doors to the infirmary cloister, a fine moulded fireplace of mid-twelfth century date with a tiled hearth, and cupboards in its walls. The room had a vault similar to that of the cellar below. Traditionally, the ground floor of the latrine block was the dayroom of the novices, outside the world of the cloister but closely connected with it. Being heated it was certainly more comfortable than the workspace provided for professed monks. There is evidence that the room was damaged by fire and a number of repairs of mid-thirteenth century date including a second fireplace (now blocked) and new doors in the north wall suggest that it was then divided up into two or more rooms with timber partitions. A single door jamb in the north wall is evidence that a cross-wall at ground floor level divided the novices' room from a latrine to the east. The east wall of this room was partially rebuilt in the late fourteenth century.

The upper floor, which occupied the full width of the building was the **monks' latrine**, with a row of privies arranged over the drain along the south wall. Sockets in the south wall suggest individual closets, but these probably date to the late-fourteenth century when the range was shortened and a new gable wall built, contemporary with the shortening of the dormitory. The latrine must have been lit from its north side as no windows exist in the south wall.

Return to the cloister from the monks' dayroom.

The south range of the cloister was substantially rebuilt in the last decades of the twelfth century and marks a departure from Aelred's original design.

WARMING HOUSE AND LATER DAY-STAIR

The easternmost room of the south cloister range was traditionally the **warming house** where a fire was kept burning from 1 November until Good Friday. At Rievaulx, it is a fine room with a great double fireplace against its west wall, a part of the rebuilding of the south cloister range in the last decade of the twelfth century. There are two doors in its north wall. One in the centre gave on to the warming house itself. Another, in the east corner originally led to a covered passage leading to the southern part of the dormitory range. This door was retained to serve **new day-stairs** to the monks' dormitory, nothing of which now remain apart from the springers of a low vault that supported it.

The warming house originally had an aisle of three bays on its south side. At first, the room was not vaulted, which must have constituted a severe fire risk. A stone vault was soon inserted, however, and the piers of the arcade strengthened with a jacket of stone. Towards the end of the fourteenth century the aisle was taken down, the arcade blocked up, and a door inserted at the west end. The recessed sills of windows survive in each bay, that to the east containing a stone sink.

There was a room above the warming house, which was probably reached from the day-stair. In 1538 this room was called 'the house for evidence' and it was fitted with great cupboards for documents. It served as the repository for the abbey's deeds and other important estate papers.

ENGLISH HERITAGE

The latrines were flushed by a branch of the River Rye which crossed the site in a culvert

23

Flanking the refectory entrance were lavers where the monks washed in pewter basins set in a wall arcade

REFECTORY

After the church, the **refectory** or dining-hall was the largest and most elaborately decorated building at the abbey and one of the most magnificent examples of the type raised in Britain. Built in the last decade of the twelfth century, its architecture breaks dramatically from the austere materials and forms used following the abbey's foundation. For much of the year the monks ate only one meal a day here, around noon. Meat was excluded from their diet and daily fare consisted of bread and usually two vegetable dishes, with beans and leeks as a staple. For certain feast days eggs, cheese and fish provided variety. Beer, brewed without hops, furnished drink.

Entrance to the refectory from the cloister lay through a single, richly moulded doorway. The refectory floor was at the cloister alley level, supported on vaults that have fallen. Flanking the doorway were the shallow stone water-troughs of the laver, lined with pewter until 1538, and topped by moulded arches supported on carved brackets. Water flowed from lead pipes into the troughs where the monks washed their hands prior to meals. Every Saturday, in addition, the laver was used for the ceremonial washing of feet, emulating the rite instituted by Christ for the Apostles immediately before the Last Supper.

The arrangements and service within the refectory followed custom. At the end furthest from the cloister was a dais on which the prior and senior monks sat, the abbot being required to eat with guests. The rest of the community occupied benches placed along the side walls facing wooden tables on stone supports. The refectory hall was a clear, unencumbered space rising to a height of 15.2m (50ft). It was composed in two parts: a lower, plain masonry wall against which the benches and tables of the monks were set; and an upper part arranged in a series of blind arches and glazed lancet windows with richly worked hood-mouldings.

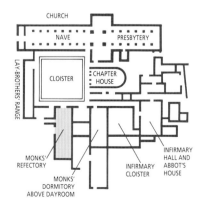

CHURCH

NAVE　　PRESBYTERY

LAY-BROTHERS' RANGE

CLOISTER　　CHAPTER HOUSE

MONKS' REFECTORY

MONKS' DORMITORY ABOVE DAYROOM

INFIRMARY CLOISTER

INFIRMARY HALL AND ABBOT'S HOUSE

Particularly notable was the reader's pulpit in the west wall. It occupied four arches within the thickness of the wall and was reached by flights of stairs.

Meals were taken in silence broken only by readings from the Bible or patristic commentaries. On the same wall, close to the cloister, is the serving hatch through which food was passed from the kitchen. At the wall head are brackets and wall-shafts that supported the timbers of the roof, as well as those inserted in the fifteenth century when Abbot William Spenser lowered the pitch of the roof. The interior of the building was covered with a pale pink lime-wash on which a masonry pattern was picked out in red paint.

This refectory replaced an earlier structure of the 1150s, of which fragments remain in the adjacent walls of the kitchen and warming house. Originally both kitchen and refectory lay

parallel to the cloister alley. When reconstructed, the refectory was turned through 90 degrees, following a plan developed in the order's other large monasteries a generation earlier.

Because of the terracing of the site, the refectory was carried on an undercroft. Construction began at the south end and progressed towards the cloister. Originally, the undercroft was designed to be vaulted in three aisles from two rows of columns. Before the work was completed, however, the design was changed and a central row of columns substituted. The old columns were re-used, but because they were required to carry more weight, the masons jacketed them with additional masonry. The undercroft was then divided into a number of rooms for storage.

TOP *The refectory and its lower-ground storey.* ABOVE *A reconstruction of the refectory, drawn by Peter Dunn. Readings were given from the pulpit, while the monks ate in silence*

25

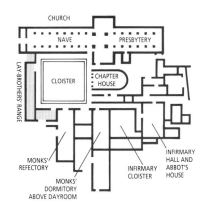

```
                    CHURCH
              NAVE        PRESBYTERY

                              CHAPTER
         CLOISTER            HOUSE
LAY-BROTHERS' RANGE


  MONKS'                          INFIRMARY
  REFECTORY                       HALL AND
                                  ABBOT'S
          MONKS'        INFIRMARY HOUSE
          DORMITORY     CLOISTER
          ABOVE DAYROOM
```

KITCHEN

Between the refectory and the west range of the cloister is the **kitchen**, a heavily ruined and complicated building that retains evidence of three phases of construction. In its present form it dates to the fourteenth century when, like the chapter house and dormitory, it was reduced in size to serve a smaller community.

The cloister wall dates to Aelred's time and retains at a high level the internal splay of a window. The opposite wall remains at the level of the lower terrace to the south, now enclosing a passage into the basement level of the refectory. This passage, an original feature of the kitchen, was covered by a vault that carried the kitchen floor and there was probably an arcade on the line of the later south wall (a feature copied in the warming house). A localised widening on the outer face of the south wall marks the position of a large fireplace added to the aisle, but the main hearth would have been in the centre of the building.

The kitchen was substantially remodelled when the new refectory was begun, with a vault inserted to fireproof the building. A cupboard and a hatch to the refectory date from this period, the hatch containing a revolving dumb-waiter by which food was passed to the servers in the refectory, a feature which can also be seen at Fountains Abbey.

In the fourteenth century, the southern aisle was demolished, and a new wall built along the line of the twelfth-century arcade. This wall contains a substantial fireplace, perhaps replacing that in the demolished outer wall. Tiled hearths in the floor also date to this period. The western part of the kitchen was walled off, perhaps to form a separate scullery. In all, the size of the kitchen itself was greatly reduced, mirroring the reduced size of the community and especially the loss of the lay-brothers, for the earlier kitchen had served their

Lay-brothers farmed the abbey's estates. The community was self-sufficient, and corn was stored in the granary

refectory in the west range as well as that of the monks. Additionally, the Cistercians had begun to eat meat in the later fourteenth century, and meat dishes were prepared in a separate kitchen and eaten in a separate refectory called the misericord, both of which normally lay outside the confines of the cloister.

WEST RANGE (LAY-BROTHERS)

The west range of the cloister in a Cistercian monastery was the home of the **lay-brothers**, containing on the ground floor the outer parlour where members of the convent could meet with outsiders, storage rooms, and the lay-brothers' refectory. The upper floor was their dormitory. At Rievaulx only the northern part of the range survives, the remainder having been demolished in the second half of the fourteenth century when it was effectively redundant. Although substantially modified from the late fourteenth century when the upper floor became a granary, a great deal of what remains is of twelfth-century date. The scale of the range suggests that it predates Aelred's rebuilding of the cloister ranges and church and that it belongs to the first phase of masonry construction in the late 1130s.

Against the church, its floor at the level of the nave floor, was the original **outer parlour** with doors to both the inner court and cloister. Its south wall also contains a door, now blocked, which was an original feature. The next four bays of the building comprised **cellarage**, though this space was divided into three rooms in the fourteenth century. The next two bays were perhaps the cellarer's office for there was a primary door in the dividing wall between it and the cellar, but in the 1190s this part of the range was substantially altered. The outer parlour was moved from the north end of the range to the site of the **cellarer's office** in about 1190 when that room was provided with a vault and new doors in the outer and cloister walls. The intention seems to have been to create a more fitting room in which the community could meet with the outside world, a room that better demonstrated the abbey's wealth and position.

Beyond, to the west, are unexcavated buildings that formed the Inner Court and controlled access to the cloister. One of these was a **conduit house** that provided piped water to the cloister ranges. To the south was a passage through the range with wide arches springing now from just above ground level in the outer and cloister walls. That in the cloister wall can still be seen, though both were later blocked. Beyond this passage, the remainder of

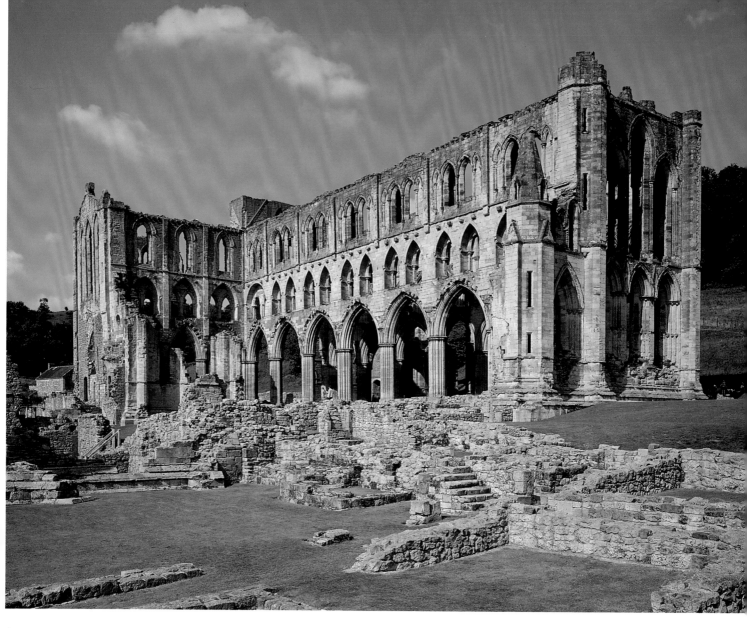

the range comprised the **lay-brothers' refectory**. Its northern end, abutting the later kitchen, was probably a servery and a door into the kitchen was provided. The **dormitory** on the floor above ran the whole length of the ground floor.

The southern part of the range must have been of three storeys like the east range because of the way it was built from the lower terrace. It was demolished in the second half of the fourteenth century. The plinth of its new gable wall survives, showing that this happened at the same time as the kitchen was being reduced in size. It was then, perhaps, that fireplaces were provided in many of the ground-floor rooms and that the new outer parlour was divided into two rooms.

From the west alley of the cloister, return to the kitchen and take the steps down to the lower terrace, passing through the basement level of the refectory. Walk around the refectory until you come to the southern extension of the east cloister range.

SOUTHERN PART OF THE EAST RANGE

Only the lower storey of Aelred's east range survives here, for the upper levels were demolished in the later fourteenth century. What remains is impressive, a great undercroft of five double bays with double-splay round-headed windows lighting each bay. Built on artificially terraced ground it appears to have suffered from subsidence from the moment it was built and to support its upper two storeys great flying buttresses were constructed. Within, groined vaults sprung from a spine wall pierced with plain round-headed arches.

The early thirteenth-century presbytery was one of the finest monastic churches in the north of England. It has remained substantially intact

27

ENGLISH HERITAGE

THE LATE MEDIEVAL ABBOT'S HOUSE

In the closing years of the fifteenth century, Abbot John Burton required a larger house than the long house could provide and converted the infirmary hall into one of the largest abbot's houses built in England. Its layout can be largely reconstructed from the surviving structure and documents that describe it in 1538/9.

A floor was inserted in the southern eight bays of the old infirmary hall, and a new door provided in the west wall, reached by a stone stair from the east cloister alley. Above the elaborate door-case is a representation of the Annunciation of the Virgin. The southern two bays contained chambers at first and second floor levels, served by a latrine tower against the outer face of the west wall. The next bay north contained the screens passage or entrance to the abbot's hall which occupied four full bays of the building. A great rectangular pier at the centre of the old infirmary supported the central hearth at the upper end of this hall. All of the windows in the west wall of the hall were remodelled as four-light square-headed windows of early Tudor type. The next two bays of the old hall were taken down and replaced by a two-storey cross-wing with a tall window in the west wall and projecting oriel windows to the east. There was a fireplace in the north wall on each floor, and the rooms can be identified; that at ground level being the abbot's parlour, with his great chamber above. The northernmost bay at first floor level contained three small rooms, one of which communicated with the infirmary chapel which now served the abbot's use. The ground floor of the old infirmary was used largely as storage or as passages through the building. Only one room, at the south east corner, was used by the abbot as his private dining chamber. Here a large fireplace was provided for his comfort.

The old abbot's house to the west was widened at first floor level to incorporate the north alley of the infirmary cloister and formed a long gallery accessible from the abbot's hall, a fashionable development seen also at Fountains Abbey, where the abbot could entertain more privately. The garth of the infirmary cloister was then converted into a garden for the abbot's enjoyment.

It could have served as a work room for the lay-brothers. A single latrine was provided in its north wall. In the sixteenth century it was the abbey's tannery and the brick and stone-built tanning vats remain along the west wall. Tanning was a noxious process and it is surprising that the monks permitted it so close to the cloister.

Very little remains of the first floor of this part of the east range. A single square pier from the central arcade survives because it had subsided below the level of the roof of the later tannery. The first floor was reached from the cloister through the passage at the east end of the south range and along a gallery that flanked the east range to a porch at the north-west corner of the room. The function of the room or rooms above the tannery is not known.

Return from here to the south alley of the cloister and take the passage through the east range at the end of the south cloister alley which leads to the infirmary cloister.

To the east side of the monks' dormitory lay the infirmary reserved for the sick and aged monks. The monks' infirmary buildings constructed about 1160 are the earliest standing at a Cistercian site in Britain and provide valuable information about planning and medical organisation. The buildings that formed this complex were remodelled in the late fifteenth century into a grand residence for the abbot.

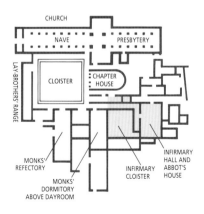

INFIRMARY CLOISTER

The infirmary had its own cloister surrounded on all four sides by open arcades. A short length has been recreated from recovered fragments in the north alley. The south and west alleys were removed in the late fifteenth century and the arcades on the north and east sides replaced by solid walls.

LONG HOUSE

To the north of the infirmary cloister was a building known in 1538 as the 'long house'. Originally built in the 1150s, it was a two-storey structure that linked the infirmary and monks' dormitory. It can be identified as the house built for Abbot Aelred whose severe illness in the last ten years of his life caused the General Chapter of the order to ordain that he reside apart from the community. Its construction followed the building of the east cloister range but was contemporary with the building of the infirmary hall. Only the ground floor remains, with a large room (partly filled

INFIRMARY HALL

Dominating the complex was the large infirmary hall of ten bays with an eastern aisle. Though the arcade wall has fallen, two of its piers with scalloped capitals have been re-erected. The hall itself was lit by tall round-headed windows that survive in the west wall, though their heads have been altered. The original arrangements can still be made out. The beds for the sick were placed in the aisle where individual bays were divided by timber screens. In the second and sixth bays from the north are original fireplaces and additional warmth was probably supplied by portable

In the mid-nineteenth century the ruins of Rievaulx Abbey were a popular subject with artists of the Romantic movement, among whom William Richardson was the first to appreciate the value of precise architectural detail

when the building was remodelled) to the west, and a square, vaulted room to the east with a door to the infirmary hall. The western room was probably the hall, with the abbot's chamber above the vaulted room to the east. It was in this building, according to his biographer Walter Daniel, the infirmarer, that Aelred wrote the literary and spiritual treatises which earned him a world-wide reputation.

Aelred's successors continued to use this building as their residence. In the thirteenth century, the floor of the western room was raised and a handsome hall constructed, lit by four pairs of lancet windows on the north side. This room was later subdivided.

braziers. In the fourth bay a door opened to the buildings that lay to the east; it aligns with a door in the west wall that led to the long house. A further door in bay seven, opposite the main door to the hall, also led east, perhaps to the kitchen, and a door in the southernmost bay led to a much altered room that was probably the twelfth-century infirmary chapel. In the south wall are two original doors that led to a building over the abbey's main drain that contained the infirmary latrine and perhaps the bath-house.

Modification of the hall began in the mid-thirteenth century. Following the completion of the new choir arm of the church, a door was

inserted in the north wall of the hall that led
through a covered gallery to a door in the south
presbytery aisle. Privacy within the infirmary
was increased by the replacement of timber
screens with stone walls to provide individual
rooms, a process which was to continue
throughout the life of the building. A new
chapel was also provided to the north-east of
the hall, raised on an undercroft which is all
that survives today. The old chapel was rebuilt,
perhaps to provide accommodation for the
infirmarer.

INFIRMARY KITCHEN

In the yard to the east of the infirmary hall are
the fragmentary remains of a large kitchen. As
they appear today, they represent the kitchen of
the abbot's house with three substantial hearths
and two ovens. Parts of the building are earlier
and may be part of an earlier kitchen serving the
infirmary.

BUILDINGS ON THE EAST SIDE
OF THE INFIRMARY YARD

Partly underlying the modern access road is a
large late twelfth-century building, remodelled
in the fourteenth century and containing at its

south end a pair of ovens. It belongs to a larger
group of buildings which in the early sixteenth
century appears to have been converted to use
as an infirmary. Although they have been
partially excavated they are not displayed.

*From here return towards the admission point on
the surfaced path. On your right are the heavily
ruined remains of the abbey's fulling mill.*

FULLING MILL

The fulling or walk mill, one of three mills
within the precinct, lay on the north bank of
the original course of the River Rye (the course
of which is now marked by a belt of trees),
within its own walled yard. Here, woollen cloth
was bleached, and wool stored for export. A
similar building is known at Fountains Abbey.

On the south side was an office with a wall
fireplace and a brick-paved dais that once
carried a desk. The base of a stair indicates that
this room had a chamber above. Sockets in the
surviving walls indicate that this building,
unlike those of the cloister, was timber-framed.
The remainder of the structure is featureless
and probably represents storage space. The
watermill itself has yet to be excavated.

ACKNOWLEDGEMENTS

The writers acknowledge with gratitude the considerable help and advice of Stuart Harrison who has made the results of his own extensive research on the upstanding fabric available to them. In addition they wish to thank the American National Endowment for the Humanities which sponsored their recent re-examination of the site, and the historical research on Rievaulx by Dr Janet Burton, who has generously provided them with important new information.

FURTHER READING

Surprisingly, scholars have paid little attention to Rievaulx Abbey, partly because it has always been undeservedly overshadowed by Fountains, and partly because it remained unexcavated until the early twentieth century. The complexity of its remains has also discouraged study. The most comprehensive account of the abbey's history and architecture is P Fergusson and S Harrison, *Rievaulx Abbey: Community, Architecture, Memory* (New Haven and London 1999).

The first analysis of the site, before its excavation, was undertaken by Sir William St John Hope and can be found in the *Victoria County History, North Yorkshire*, I (Oxford 1914) pp 494-99. A more recent survey can be found in Sir Nikolaus Pevsner, *The Buildings of England, North Riding* (London 1966) pp 299-303. The importance of Rievaulx in the development of Cistercian architecture is examined in P J Fergusson, *Architecture of Solitude, Cistercian Abbeys in 12th Century England* (Princeton 1984), and a discussion of the earliest buildings can be found in R Halsey, 'The earliest architecture of the Cistercians in England' in C Norton and D Park (ed) *Cistercian Art and Architecture in England* (Cambridge 1986) pp 65-85.

The late twelfth-century refectory is described in P J Fergusson, 'The twelfth century refectories at Rievaulx and Byland Abbeys' in ibid pp 160-180. The layout of the abbey in 1538, recovered from contemporary documents, is discussed by G Coppack in 'Some descriptions of Rievaulx Abbey in 1538/9, the disposition of a major Cistercian precinct' in *Journal of the British Archaeological Association*, 139 (1986), pp 100–33.

The development of the precinct and the quarrying of stone for building are examined in H A Rye 'Rievaulx Abbey, its canals and building stones' in the *Archaeological Journal* 57 (1900), pp 69-77, and in J Weatherill, 'Rievaulx Abbey: the stone used in its building' in *Yorkshire Archaeological Journal* 38 (1952-5), pp 333–54. Both of these sources are of historiographical interest only because recent research has shown that some of their conclusions are no longer valid. The only easily accessible source of information on the abbey's estates is J C Atkinson (ed), *Chartularium Rievallense, Surtees Society* 83 (1889), where Latin transcriptions of the late twelfth-century cartulary are presented with copious notes and a useful introduction. For Aelred, the standard source is F M Powicke, *The Life of Aelred of Rievaulx* by Walter Daniel (London 1950).

The ruins of Rievaulx in the 1840s, a lithograph from a watercolour by William Richardson

ENGLISH HERITAGE

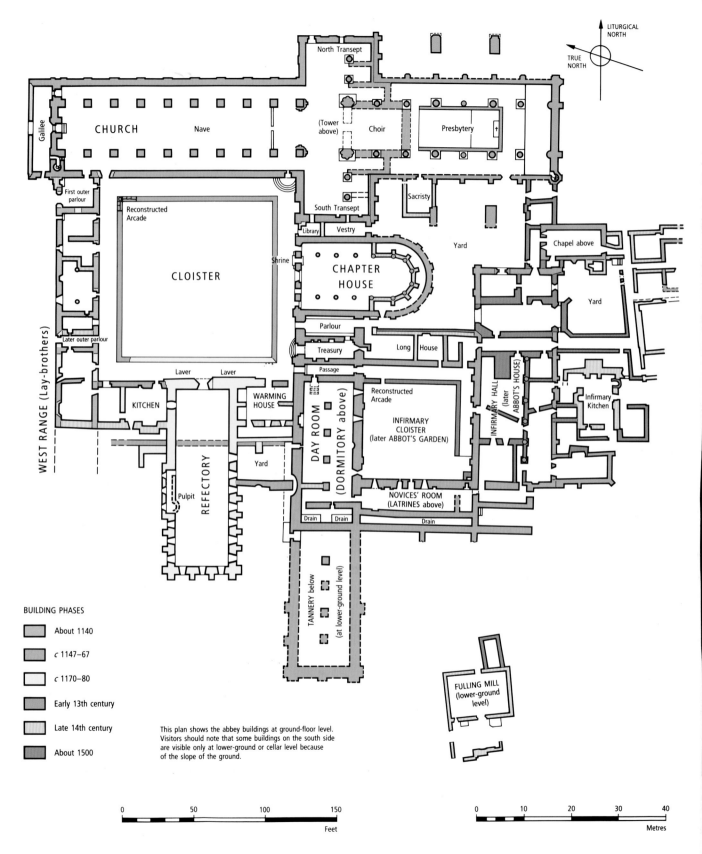

LITURGICAL
NORTH

TRUE
NORTH

North Transept

CHURCH   Nave   (Tower above)   Choir   Presbytery

Galilee

First outer parlour

Reconstructed Arcade

Sacristy

South Transept

Library   Vestry

Shrine

CLOISTER

Yard

Chapel above

CHAPTER HOUSE

Yard

Parlour

Later outer parlour

Treasury   Long   House

WEST RANGE (Lay-brothers)

Laver   Laver

Passage

KITCHEN   WARMING HOUSE

DAY ROOM (DORMITORY above)   Reconstructed Arcade   INFIRMARY CLOISTER (later ABBOT'S GARDEN)   INFIRMARY HALL (later ABBOT'S HOUSE)   Infirmary Kitchen

REFECTORY   Yard

Pulpit

NOVICES' ROOM (LATRINES above)

Drain   Drain   Drain

TANNERY below (at lower-ground level)

BUILDING PHASES

About 1140

c 1147–67

c 1170–80

Early 13th century

Late 14th century

About 1500

This plan shows the abbey buildings at ground-floor level. Visitors should note that some buildings on the south side are visible only at lower-ground or cellar level because of the slope of the ground.

FULLING MILL (lower-ground level)

0   50   100   150
Feet

0   10   20   30   40
Metres